Retro Airplanes

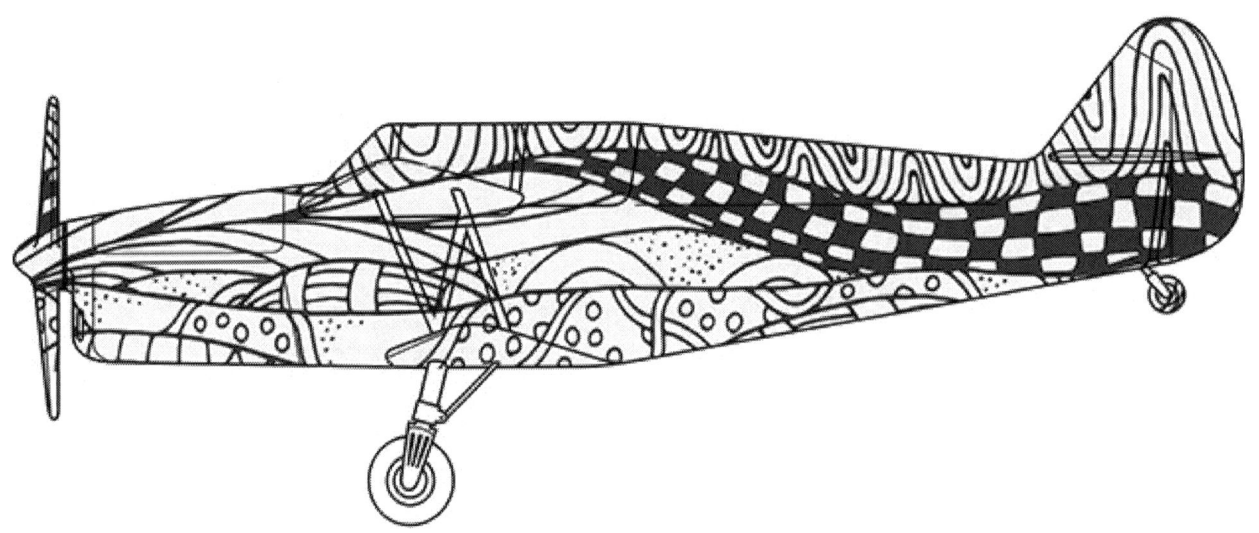

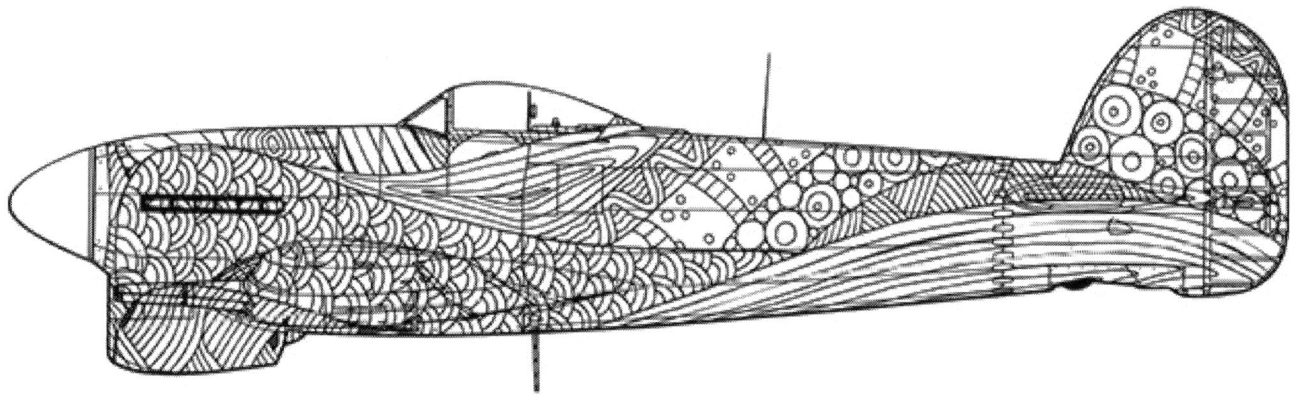

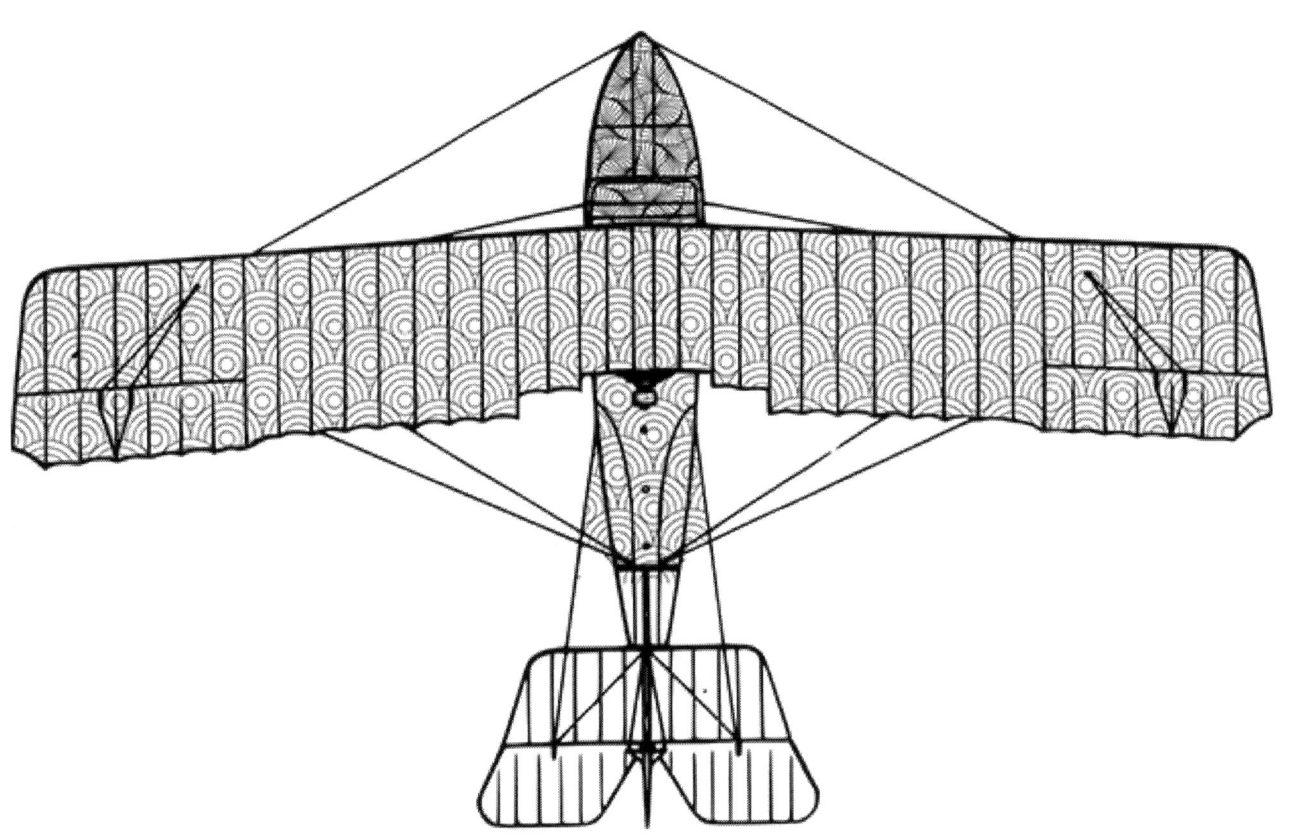

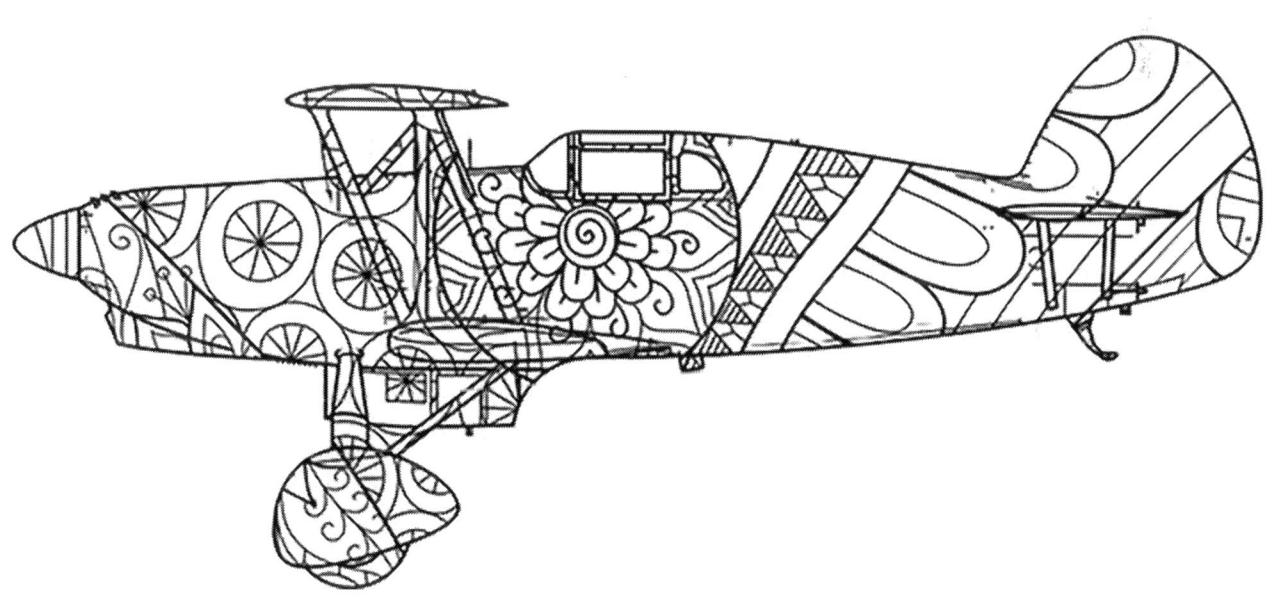

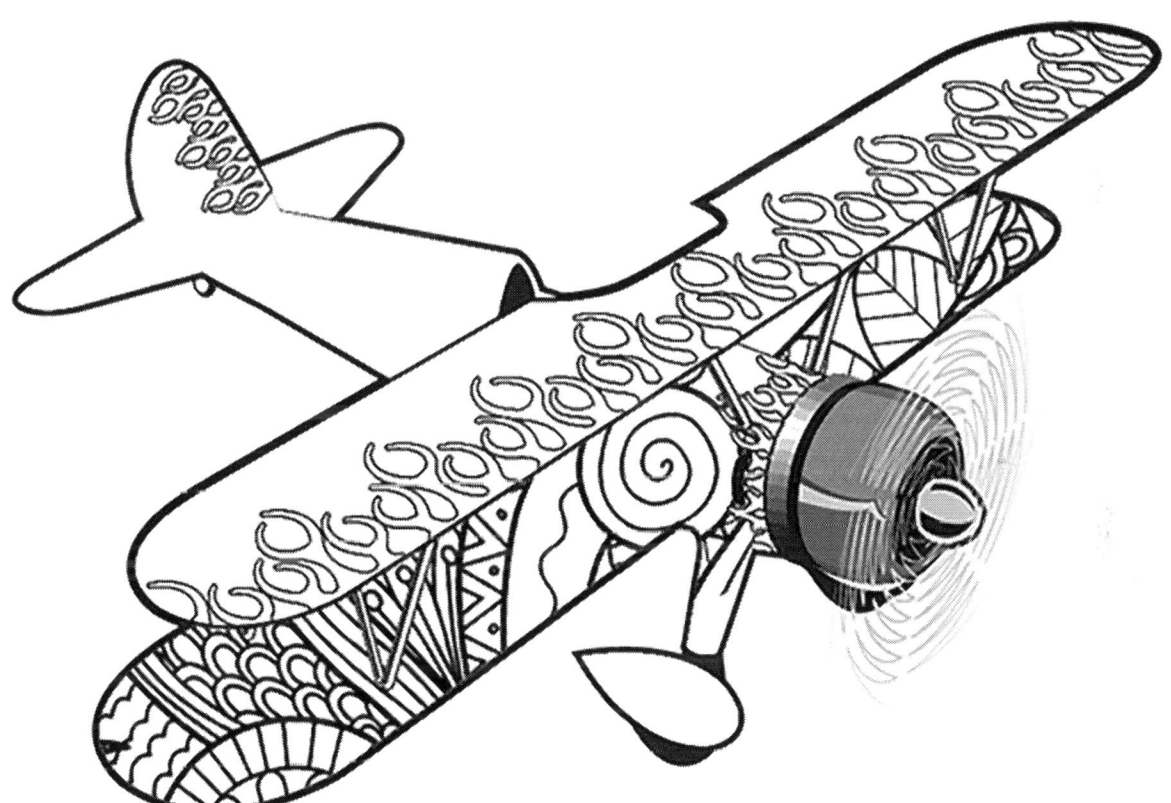

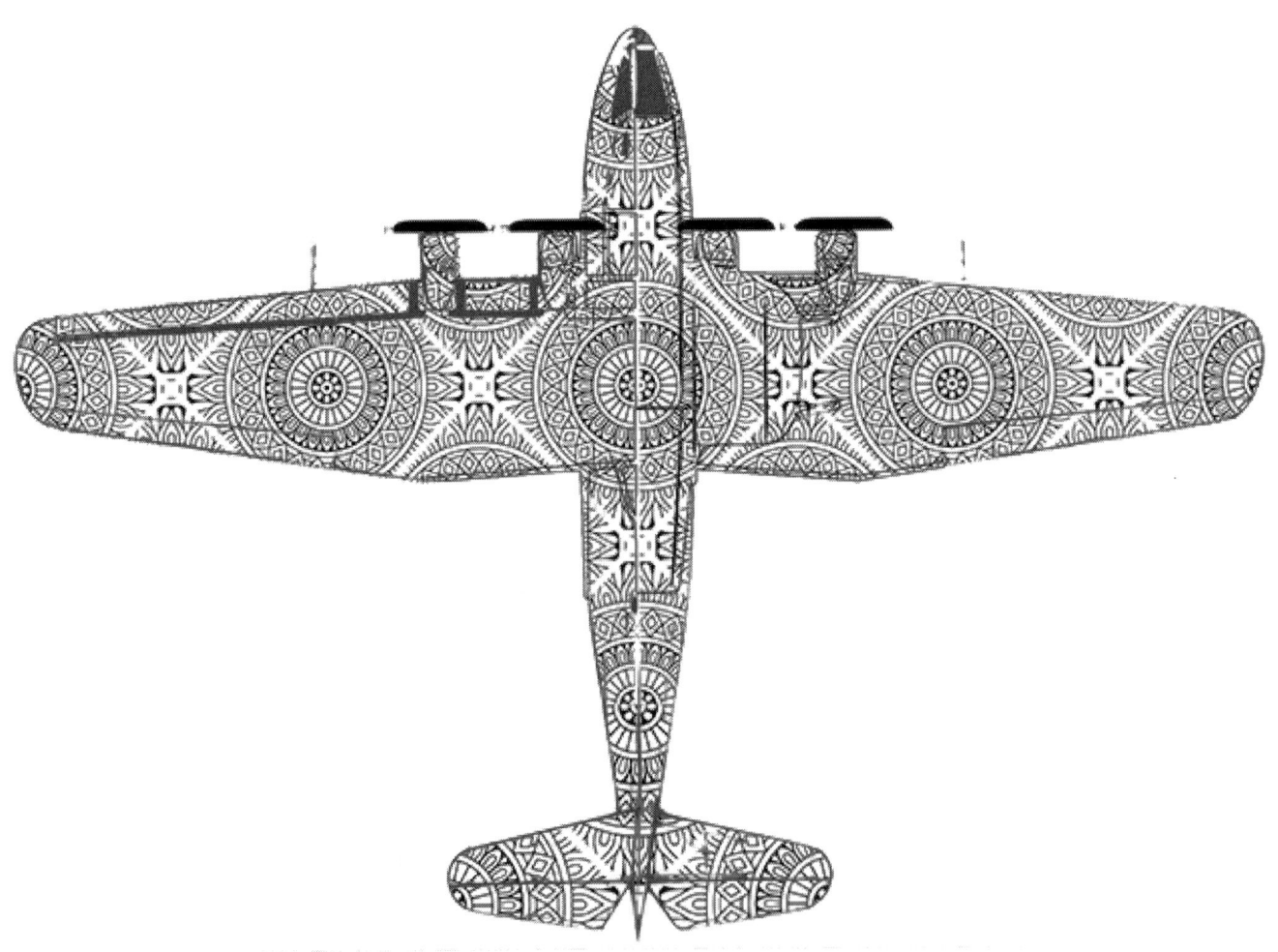

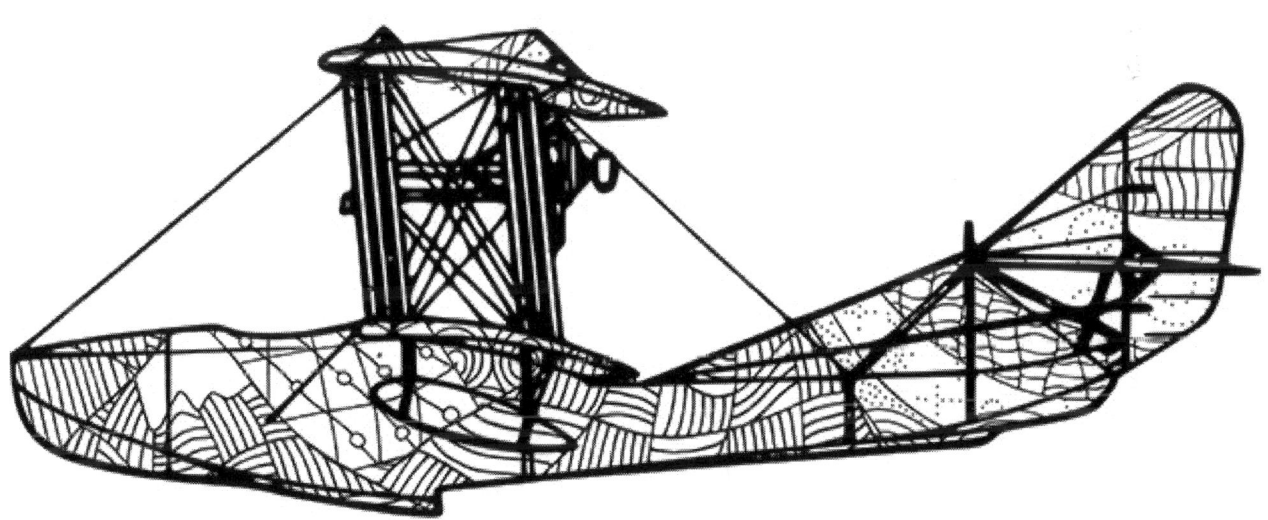

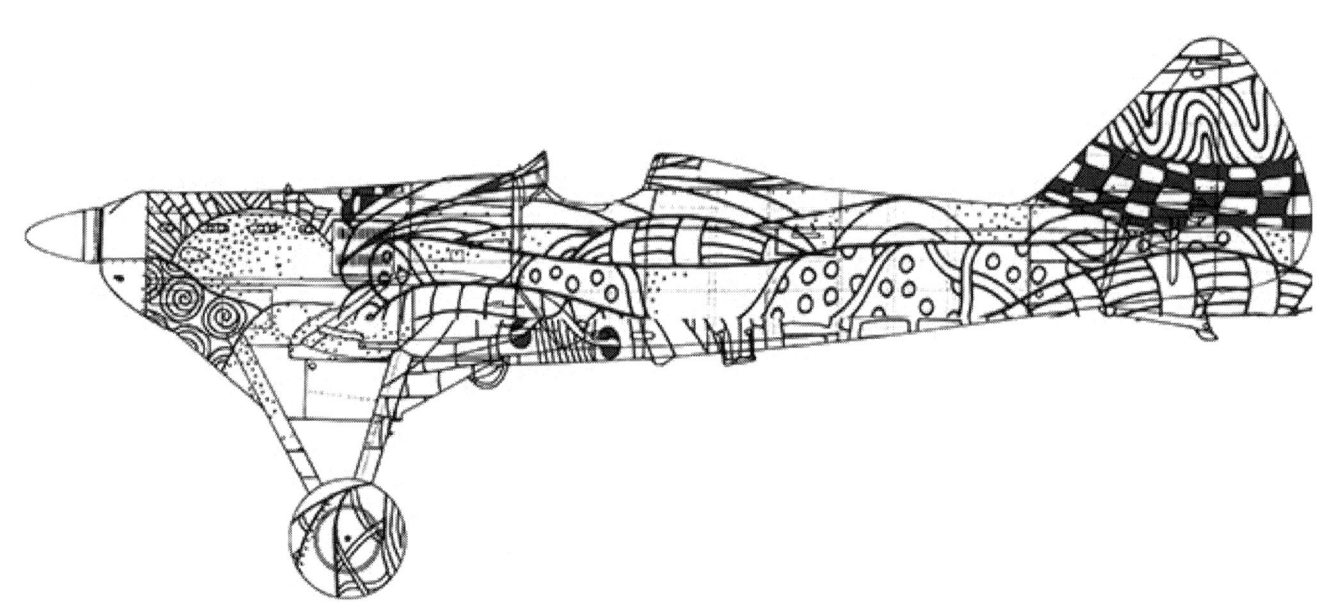

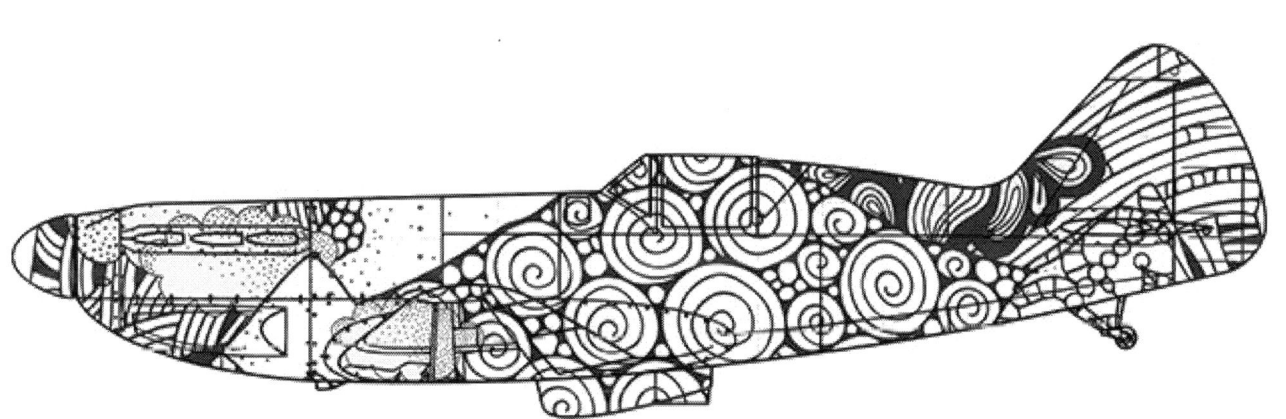

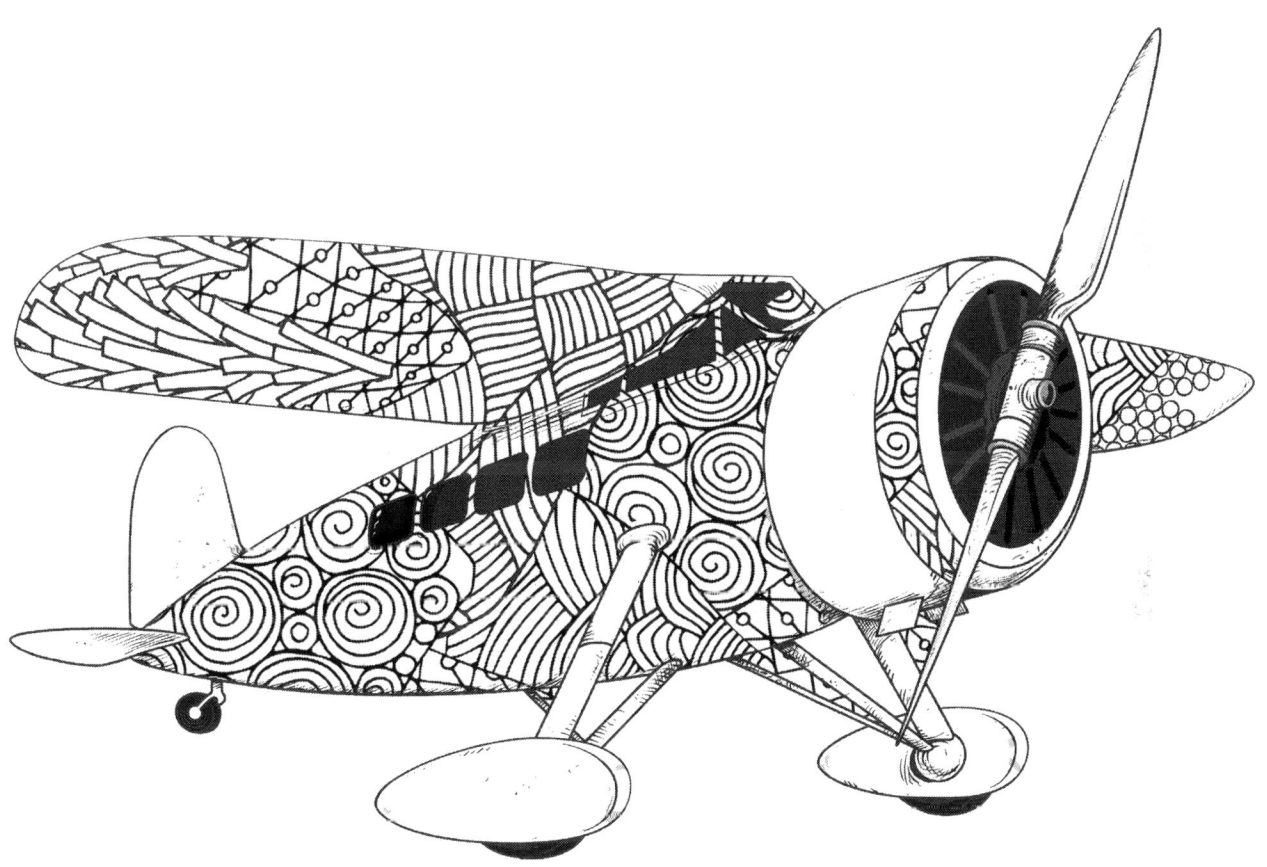

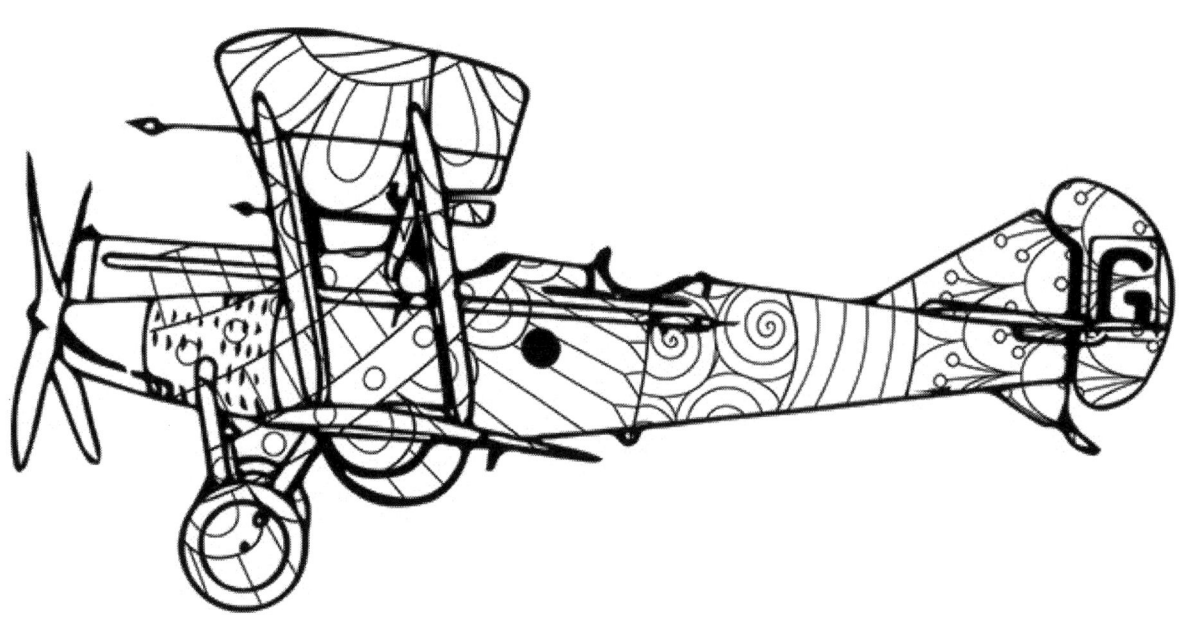

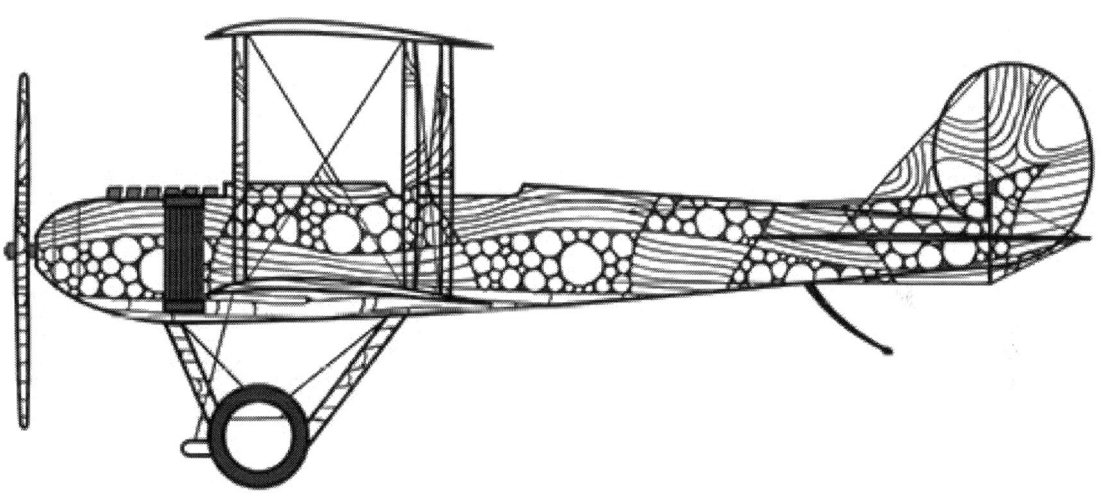

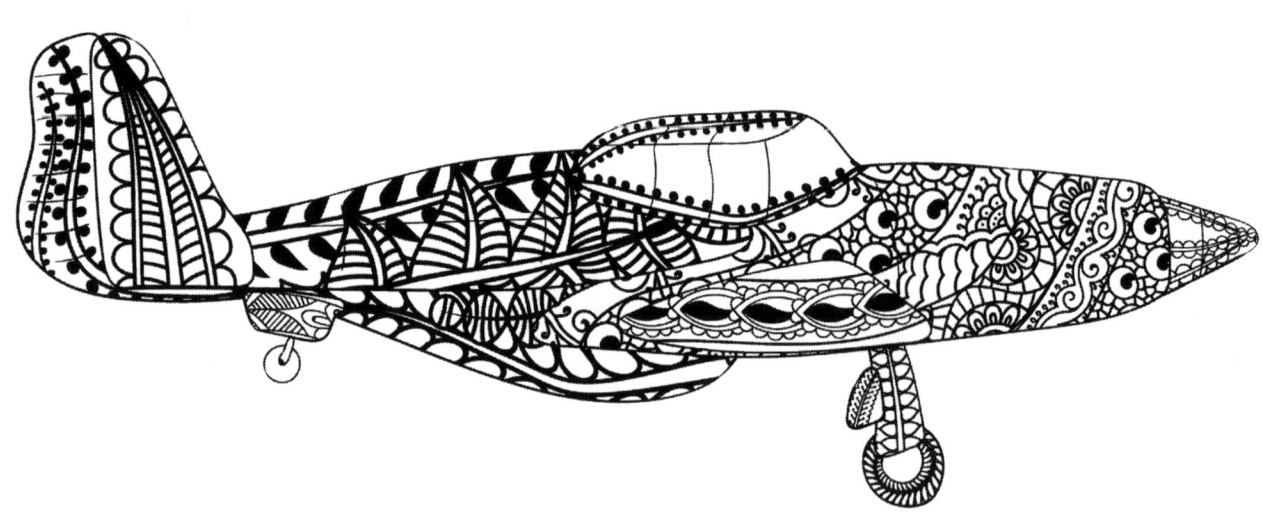

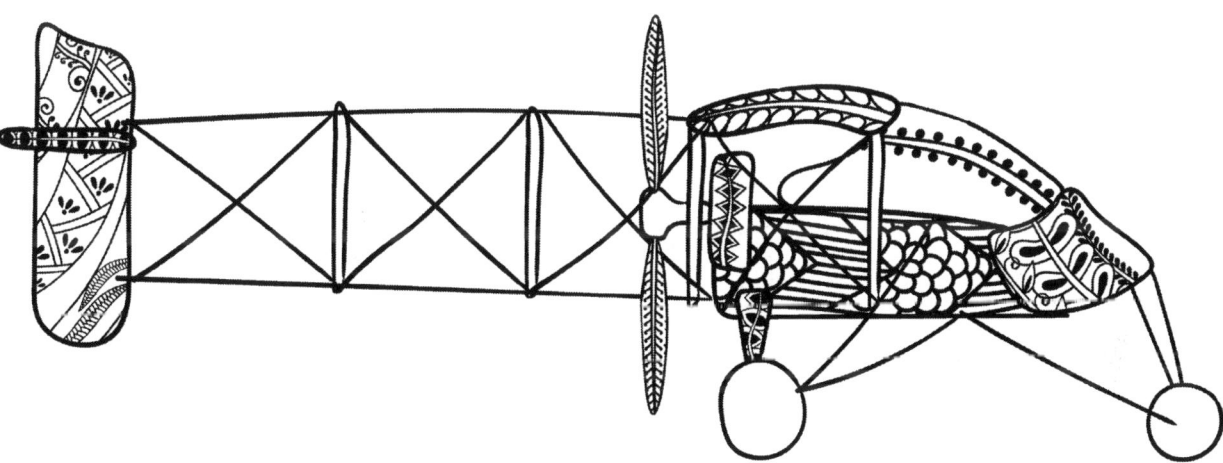

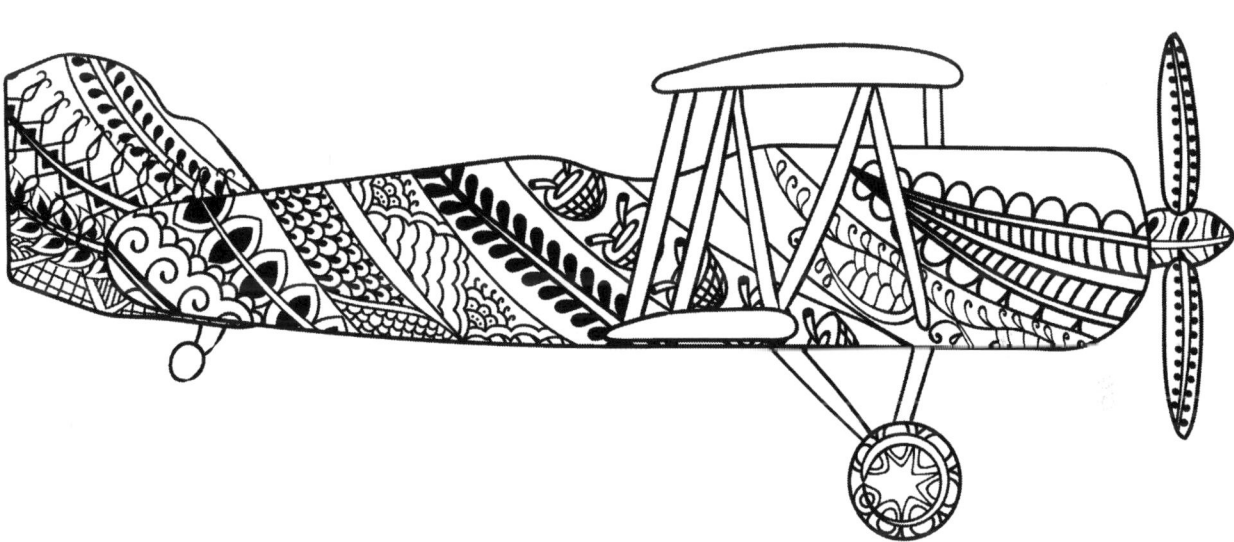

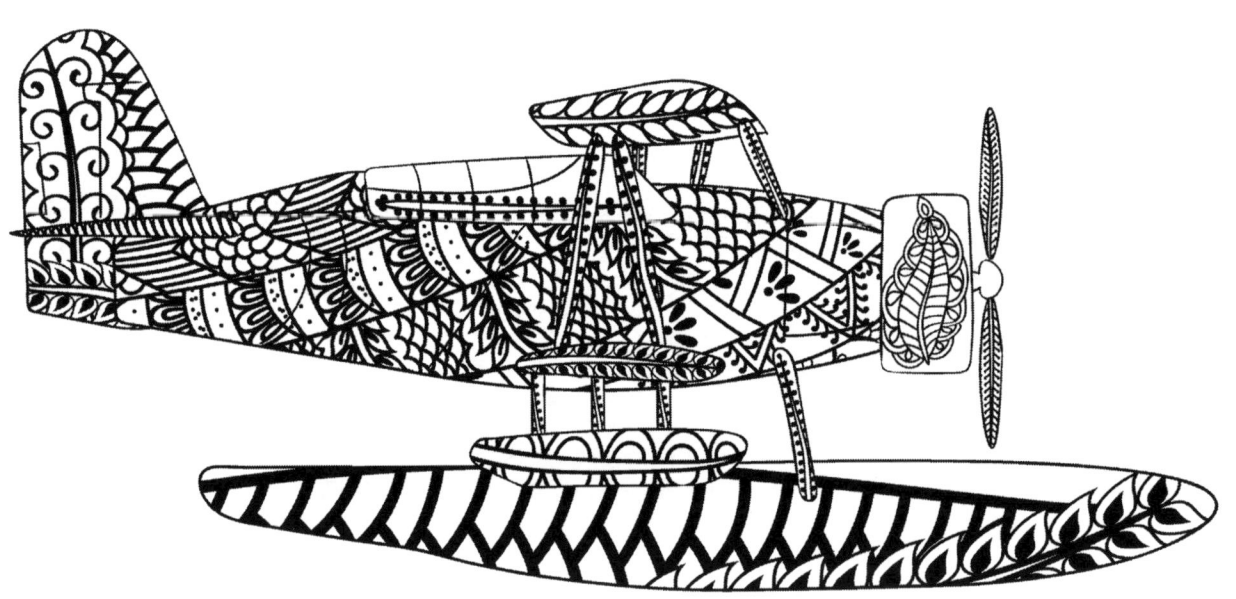

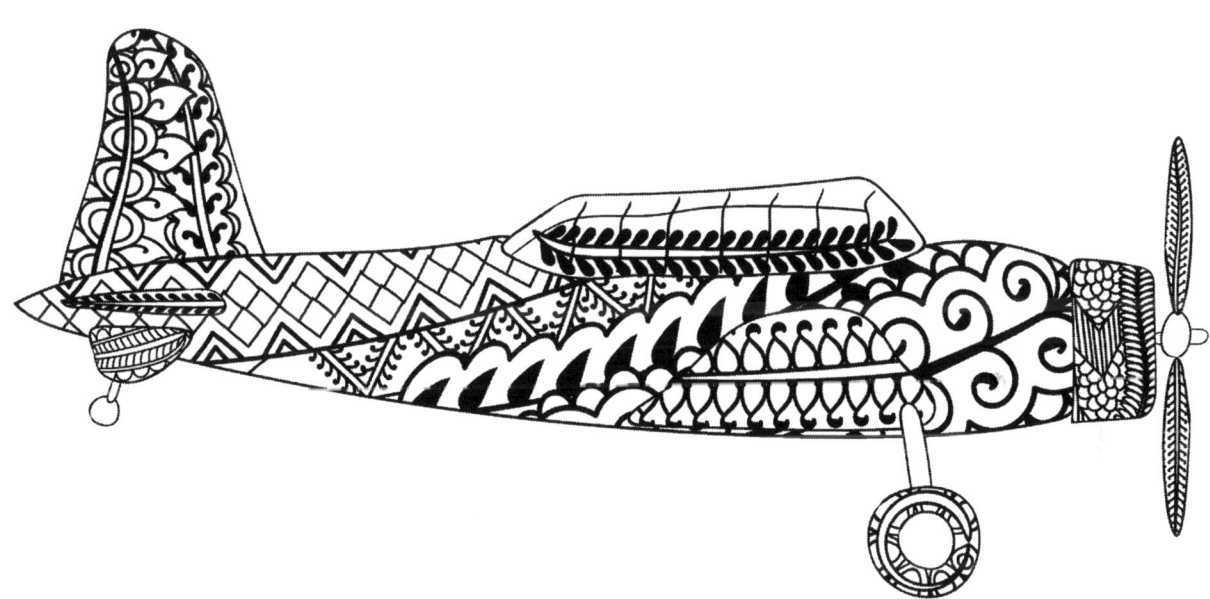

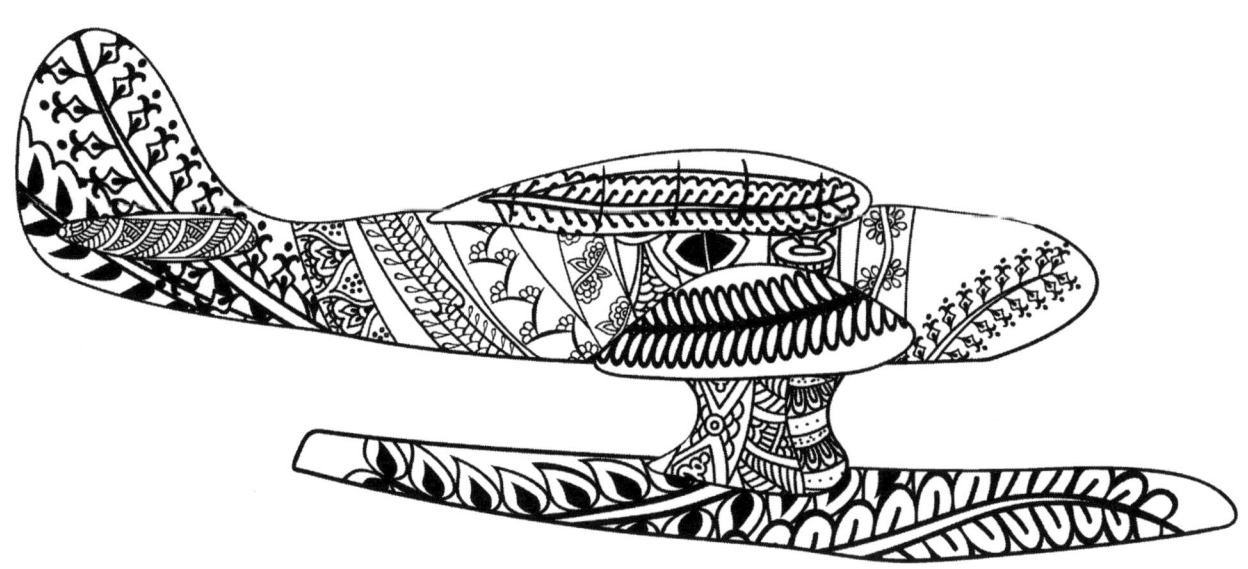

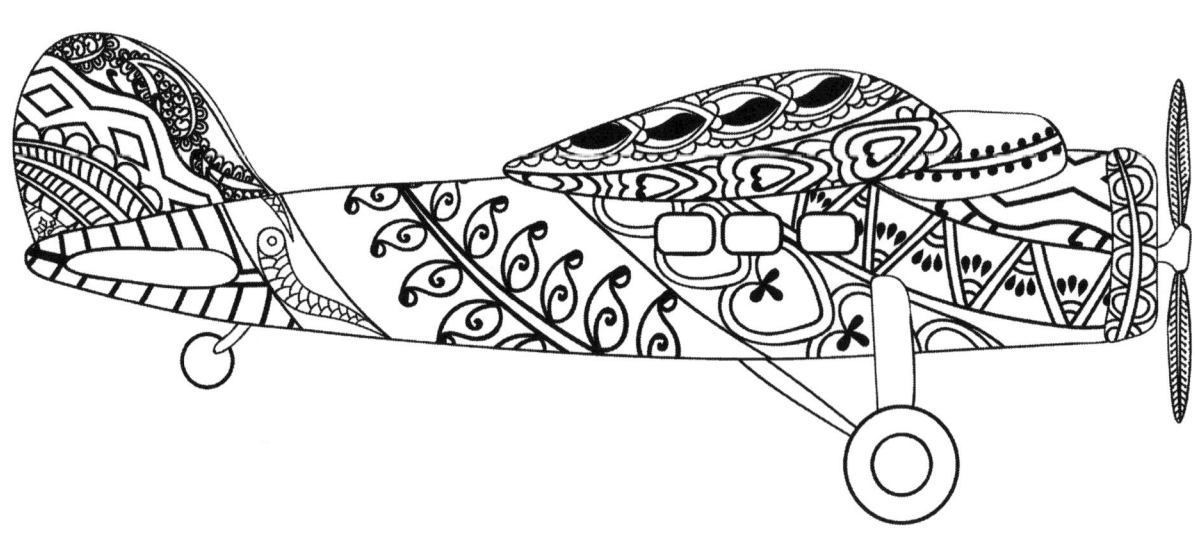

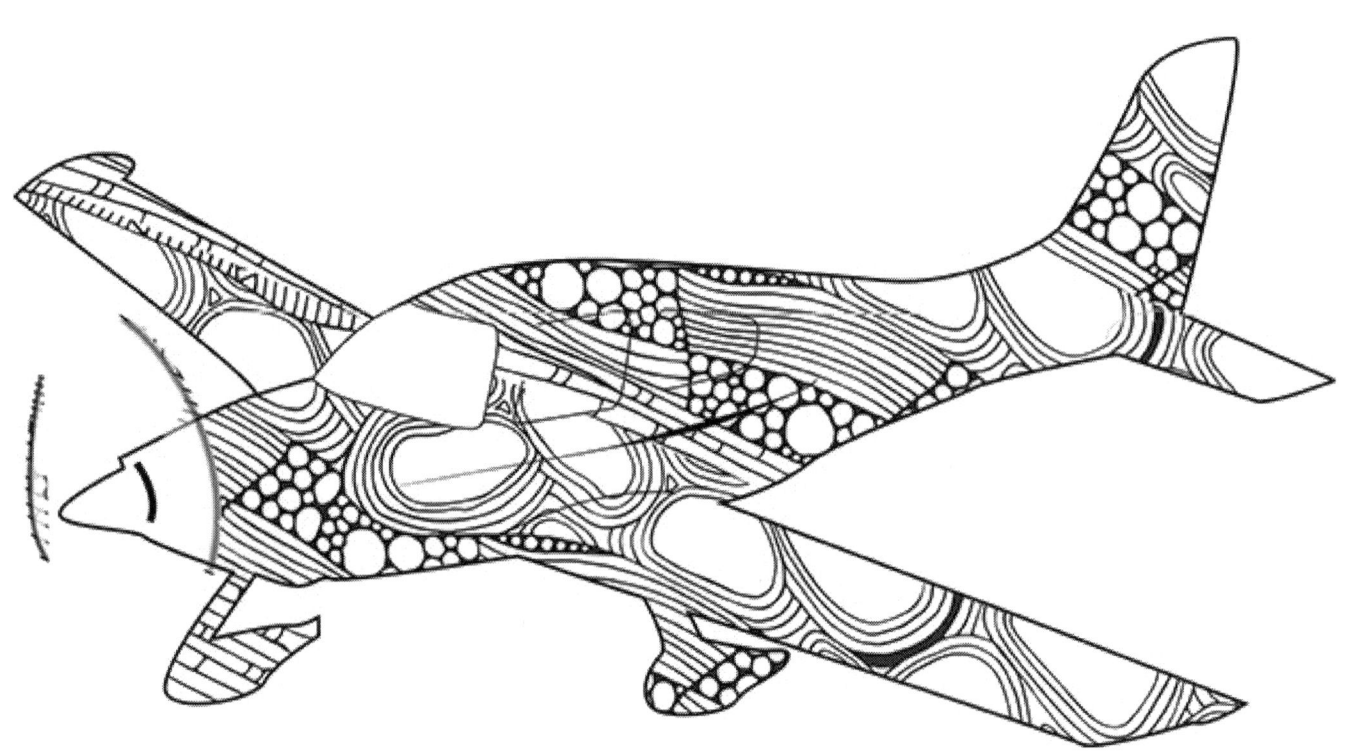

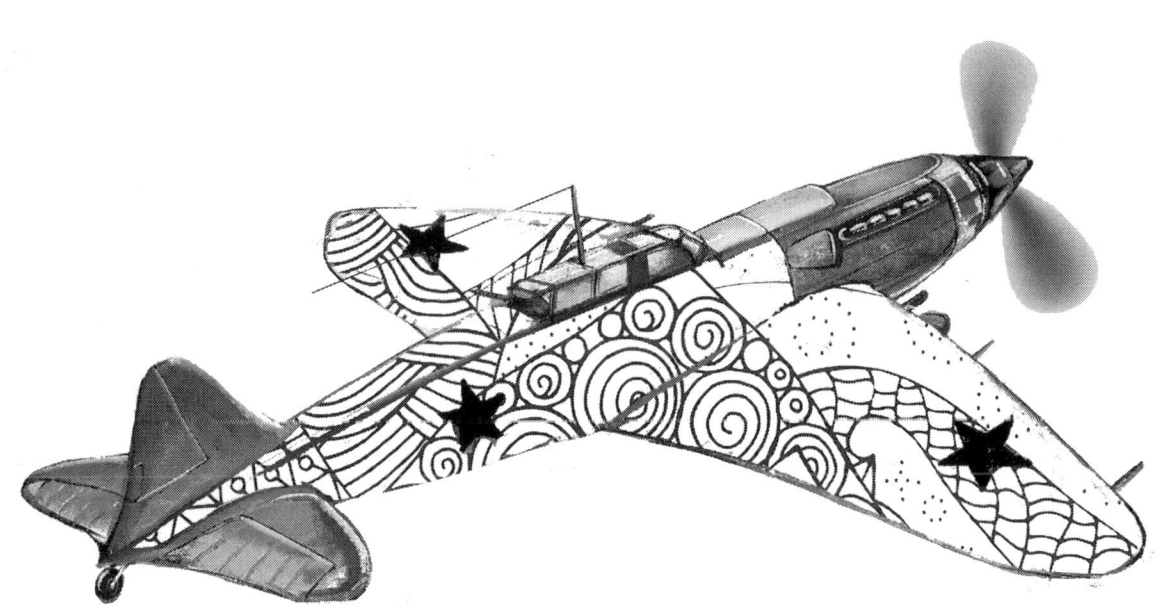

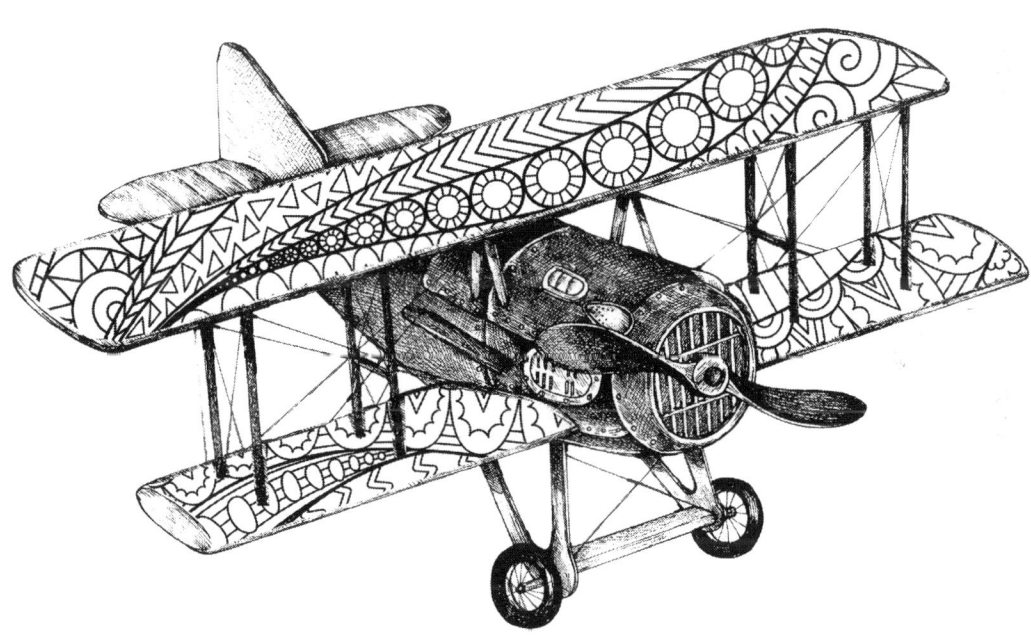

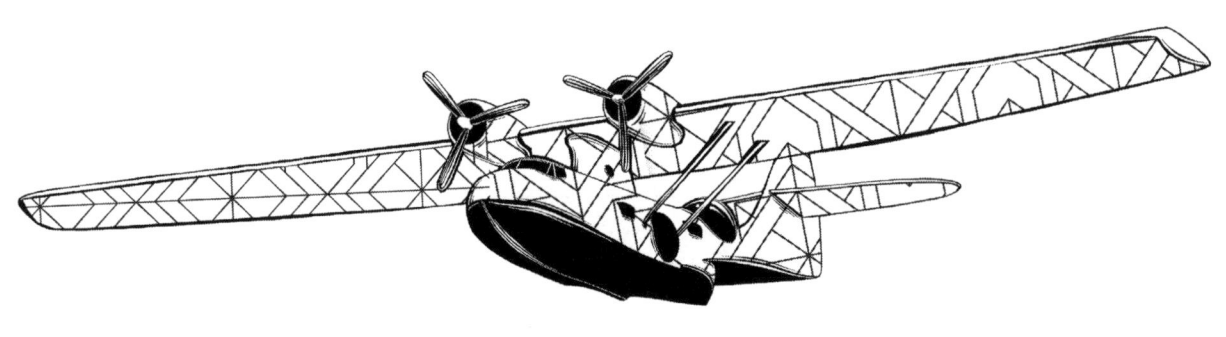

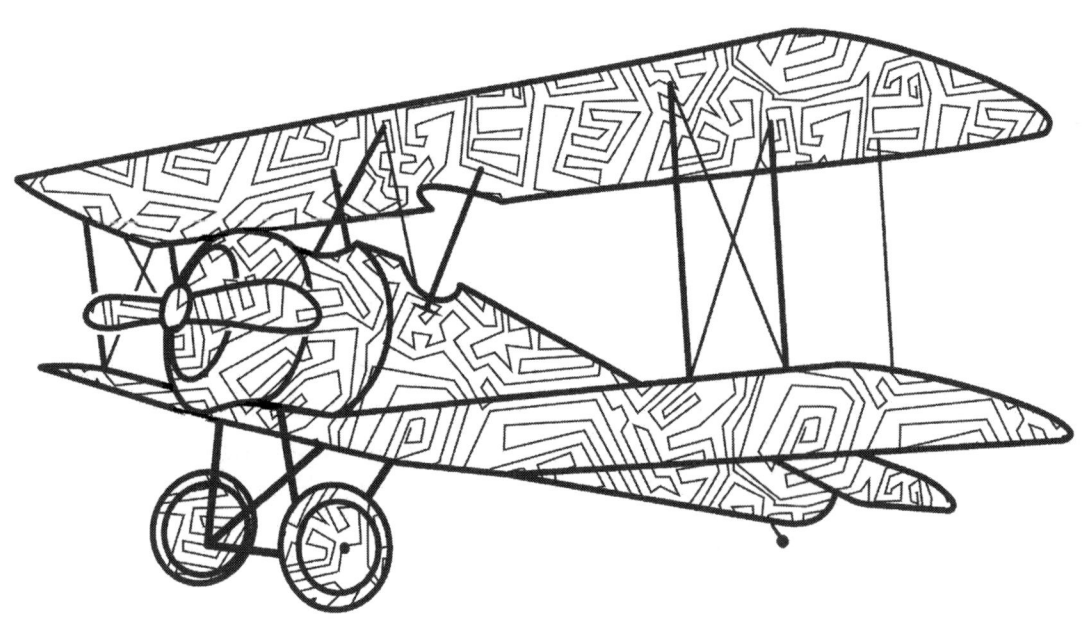

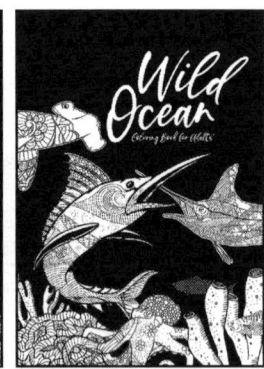

IMPRESSUM - IMPRINT
Musterstück Grafik
by Sonja Lidl
Hermannstr. 55
Germany, 12049 Berlin
info@musterstueck-grafik.de
www.musterstueck-grafik.de
www.facebook.com/musterstueck
Tax Number Steuer Nr.
35/084/02098

Made in the USA
Coppell, TX
22 November 2020